Selected Poems of Rubén Darío

The Texas Pan-American Series

RUBÉN DARÍO, 1911   *Portrait by Vázquez Díaz*

Selected Poems of Rubén Darío

Translated by LYSANDER KEMP

PROLOGUE BY OCTAVIO PAZ

Illustrations by John Guerin

UNIVERSITY OF TEXAS PRESS, AUSTIN

The Texas Pan-American Series is published with the assistance of a revolving publication fund established by the Pan-American Sulphur Company and other friends of Latin America in Texas. Publication of this book was also assisted by a grant from the Rockefeller Foundation through the Latin American translation program of the Association of American University Presses.

Type set by Service Typographers, Inc., Indianapolis
Printed by Taylor Press, Inc., Dallas
Bound by Universal Bookbindery, Inc., San Antonio

TRANSLATOR'S NOTE

In selecting the poems for this book, I have attempted to represent the whole range of Darío's verse. In translating them, I have attempted to capture something of their effect, their "feel," in what I hope is readable English. When these two aims were in conflict, I gave preference to the latter, omitting several important poems which I could not render with any degree of success, and including some minor poems which seemed to withstand the change of language more effectively.

The Prologue has been derived from a very much longer essay on Darío and Modernism, "The Seashell and the Siren," by Octavio Paz. In joining together the portions which I thought to be most helpful to the United States reader, I have translated from the original, adding only a few transitional or explanatory phrases. I am very grateful to Sr. Paz for allowing me to make and use this patchwork version.

I wish to thank George Schade, Adalberto Navarro Sánchez, and Silvio Villavicencio for their help with several problems of selection and interpretation.

Lysander Kemp

PROLOGUE

by Octavio Paz

According to the textbooks, the sixteenth and seventeenth centuries were the Golden Age of Spanish literature. Juan Ramón Jiménez has said that they were not gold but gilded cardboard. It would be fairer to say that they were the centuries of Spanish rage. During that period the Spaniards wrote, painted, and dreamed in the same frenzy in which they destroyed and created nations. Everything was carried to extremes: they were the first to circumnavigate the earth, and at the same time they were the inventors of quietism. They raged with a thirst for space, a hunger for death. Lope de Vega was prolific, even profligate: he wrote something over one thousand plays. San Juan de la Cruz was temperate, even miserly: his poetical works consist of three longish lyrics and a few songs and ballads. It was a delirium, whether boisterous or reserved, bloodthirsty or pious. The lucid delirium of Cervantes, Velázquez, Calderón. Quevedo's labyrinth of conceits. Góngora's jungle of verbal stalactites.

And then, quite suddenly, the stage was bare, as if the whole performance had been illusions rather than historical reality. Nothing was left, or nothing but ghostly reflections. During all of the eighteenth century there was no Swift or Pope, no Rousseau or Leclos, anywhere in Spanish literature. In the second half of the nineteenth century a few faint signs of life began to appear—for instance, Bécquer, whom Rubén Darío imitated in his early *Rhymes*—but there was no one to compare with Coleridge, Hölderlin, Leopardi, no one who resembled Baudelaire. And then, toward the close of the century, everything changed again, just as suddenly, just as violently. The new writers had not been expected (most certainly they had not been invited) and at first their voices were drowned out by the jeers. But a few years later, through the efforts of the very figures whom the "serious" critics had called Frenchified outsiders, the Spanish language was on its feet, was alive again. It was not as opulent as it had been during the Baroque period, but it was stronger, clearer, better controlled.

The last major Baroque poet was a Mexican nun, Sor Juana Inés de la Cruz. Two centuries later, the revival of Spanish literature—and of the language itself—was also accomplished, or at least begun, here in the New World. The movement known as Modernism, of which Rubén Darío became the leader, had a double importance in the literature of the Spanish-speaking world. On the one hand, it produced four or five poets who linked up the great chain that had come apart at the end of the seventeenth century. On the other hand, to change metaphors, it smashed windows and broke doors so that the fresh air of the times could revive the dying language. Modernism was not merely a school of poetry: it was also a dancing class, a gymnasium, a circus, and a masked ball. Ever since, Spanish has been able to put up with the most raucous noises, the most dangerous escapades. And the influence of Modernism has not ended: everything written in Spanish afterward has been affected in one way or another by that great renascence.

Modernism began in about 1880 and flourished until about 1910. With two or three minor exceptions, Spanish and Spanish-American Romanticism had given us little work of any note, and its poets never realized what Romanticism really signified. In Spanish it was merely a school of rebellion and oratory: it lacked the essential Romantic belief in the superiority of poetic vision over religious revelation. It also lacked irony, and an awareness of the relation between dreaming and waking, and a presentiment that reality is a constellation of symbols. Above all, it lacked a sense of the divided self and its desire for unity. When Romanticism flickered out, there was nothing left, and Spanish literature was reduced to speechmaking or chitchat, to the academy or the café.

France was the main source of inspiration for Spanish Romanticism. It is true that French Romanticism produced few poets comparable with those of Germany and England, but the succeeding generation gave us a cluster of works in which the Romantic aims were both consummated and transcended. Baudelaire and his followers gave Romanticism "significant form." What is even more important, they made poetry a total experience, at once verbal and spiritual. During the last third of the nineteenth century the frontiers of poetry—the frontiers of the unknown—were undoubtedly to be found in France. But despite their nearness, or perhaps because of it, Spanish writers refused to be attracted; while the Spanish Americans, weary of the pretentious prattle that emanated from Madrid, turned almost instinctively to Paris. They understood that no one can say anything personal, individual, in a language which has lost the secret of change and surprise. They sensed their differences with the Spaniards, but when they looked to France they were not in search of another world but rather of a new way of speaking.

At first, Modernism was not an organized movement. There were isolated poets in widely separated parts of the Americas, from Darío, then in Chile, to the Cuban José Martí in his New York exile. They soon came to know each other, however, and to realize that their individual efforts were part of a general change in sensibility and language. Little by little they formed groups and published their own magazines, and the various tendencies united in a movement that had two centers of activity, Buenos Aires and Mexico City. The period has been called the "second generation" of Modernism, with Rubén Darío as the bridge between the two periods. The premature death of most of the precursors, plus his gifts as critic and stimulant, made him the acknowledged leader of the movement. With increasing clarity the new poets understood that their work was the first truly independent expression in Spanish-American literature. They were not intimidated when traditional critics called them outsiders: they knew that no one finds himself until after he has left his birthplace.

The French influence was not exclusive—for example, José Martí knew and loved English and United States literature—but it was predominant. The first Modernists turned from the French Romantics to the Parnassians. The second generation, while not abandoning what had been learned from the Parnassians, turned to the Symbolists. Their interest was intense and extensive, but often their very enthusiasm clouded their judgment. They were equally impressed by Gautier and Mendès, by Heredia and Mallarmé. This is made especially clear in the series of literary portraits that Darío published in an Argentine newspaper: Poe, Villiers de l'Isle Adam, Leon Bloy, Nietzsche, Verlaine, Rimbaud, and Lautrèamont are jumbled together with minor or now-forgotten writers. It is necessary, of course, to add other names to the list: first, Baudelaire, and second, Jules Laforgue, both of them decisive in the development of the second Modernist generation; the Belgian Symbolists; and among others, Stefan George, Wilde, and Swinburne. Whitman should also be mentioned, not as a direct model but as an example and stimulus. Although his idols were not all French, Darío once said—perhaps to annoy the Spanish critics who accused him of "mental Gallicism"—that "Modernism is nothing else but Castilian prose and verse passed through the fine sieve of good French prose and verse." But it would be a mistake to reduce the movement to an outright imitation of France. The originality of Modernism does not lie in its mastery of influences but in its own creations.

As they searched for a modern, cosmopolitan language, the Spanish-American poets, by a process that looks intricate but was actually natural, rediscovered the genuine, central Spanish tradition—rhythmic versification—which is something quite different from what the traditionalists were defending. The wealth of rhythm in Modernist poetry is unique in the history of the Spanish language, and among other things it opened the way for free verse and the prose poem. Their rediscovery of the true tradition was far from casual, and what they discovered was not merely a rhetoric: it was also an aesthetic and, above all, a way of looking at the world, a way of feeling it, knowing it, and speaking of it. The Modernists accomplished more than a job of restoration; they added something new. The world, the universe, is a system of correspondencies under the rule of rhythm. Everything connects, everything rhymes. Every form in nature has something to say to every other. The poet is not a maker of rhythm but its transmitter. Analogy is the highest expression of the imagination. This longing for cosmic unity is an essential characteristic of the Modernist poet. So, too, is his fascination with cosmic diversity. Forms, colors, and sounds all fly apart; feelings and meanings come together. Poetic images are expressions, both spiritual and sensory, of that single-plural rhythm. It has been said that Modernism is a poetry of sheer emotion. I think it would be more accurate to say that the Modernist poet, despite his sometimes annoying egoism, was speaking, not of his own soul, but of that of the world as a whole.

To repeat, Rubén Darío was the bridge between the precursors and the second generation of Modernism. His constant travels and his generous activity in behalf of others made him the point of connection for the many scattered poets and groups on two continents. He not only inspired and captained the battle; he was also its observer and critic. The evolution of his poetry, from *Blue* to *Poem of Autumn*, corresponds with that of the movement, which began with him and ended with him. But his work did not end with Modernism: he went beyond it, beyond the language of that school and, in fact, of every school.

Darío was not only the richest and most ample of the Modernist poets: he was one of the great modern poets. At times, he reminds us of Poe; at other times, of Whitman. Of the first, in that portion of his work in which he scorns the world of the Americas to seek an otherworldly music; of the second, in that portion in which he expresses his vitalist affirmations, his pantheism, and his belief that he was, in his own right, the bard of Latin America as Whitman was of Anglo-America.

Darío loved and imitated Verlaine's poetry above all other, but his best poems have little resemblance to those of his model. He has superabundant health and energy; his sun is stronger, his wine more generous. Verlaine was a Parisian provincial, Darío was a Central American globetrotter. His poetry is virile: backbone, heart, sex. It is clear and rotund even when it is sorrowful. It is the work of a Romantic who was also a Parnassian and a Symbolist. The work of a hybrid, not only because of the variety of his spiritual and technical influences but also because of the very blood that flowed in his veins: Indian, Spanish, with a few drops of African. A phenomenon. A pre-Columbian idol. A hippogriff.

He was born in Metapa, a village in Nicaragua, on the eighteenth of January, 1867. He was baptized Félix Rubén García Sarmiento, but from the age of fourteen he signed his name Rubén Darío. A name that is like an expanding horizon: Persia, Judea—[1] He was precocious: innumerable poems, stories, and articles, all of them imitations of current literary fashions. The civic themes of Spanish and Spanish-American Romanticism: progress, democracy, anticlericalism, independence, Central American unity. And the lyric themes: love, the beyond, the landscape, Arabian and Gothic legends.

In 1886 Darío set out on his first trip, to Chile. The great travels had begun, and would not end until his death. In Chile he wrote his first manifestoes; at the same time he continued to

---

[1] In English, Rubén is Reuben, Darío is Darius. (Tr.)

write pallid imitations of Spanish Romanticism. But these imitations were only a farewell, because his aesthetics had already changed: "Words should paint the color of a sound, the aroma of a star; they should capture the very soul of things." In 1888 he published *Blue*, which contained both poems and stories, and which marks the official birth of Modernism. The prose was more daring than the poetry, and created a greater scandal. The unusual rhythms, the glittering words, the sensual phrasing, the insolent manner, everything was certain to irritate many readers and to enchant others. In its time, *Blue* was revolutionary and prophetic. Today, it is an historical curiosity.

Darío returned to Central America in 1889. He married, spent two months in Spain, returned. His wife died, he remarried, the marriage was a failure. In 1893 he set out again, this time for Buenos Aires—he had been appointed Colombian Consul there—but he arrived via New York, where he met José Martí, and Paris. The visit to Paris was especially important: he departed swearing by "the gods of the new Parnassus." He had met "that agèd faun, Verlaine," and he had learned something of "the mystery of Mallarmé." In Buenos Aires he found the lively, cosmopolitan, luxurious atmosphere he was seeking. The pampas and the sea, barbarism and the European mirage: it was a city suspended in time rather than fixed in space. The young writers had already made Darío's new aesthetics their own, and gathered around him almost as soon as he arrived. He was the undisputed leader. A period of agitation, polemics, dissipation. The editorial room, the restaurant, the bar. A period of creation: *Profane Hymns and Other Poems* in 1896, as well as his literary portraits. *Profane Hymns* is the book that best defines the earlier Modernism: noonday, the *ne plus ultra* of the movement. After it, the routes came to an end, one could only drop sail or voyage off into the unknown. Darío chose the former, chose to colonize the newly discovered regions.

There was a certain incompatibility between the aesthetics of *Profane Hymns* and Darío's temperament. He was sensual, many-sided, gregarious, never a hermit. He was lost in the worlds of the world but he never withdrew into contemplation of his own self. What gives unity to the book is not its ideas but its feelings. It is a unity of accent and tone, very different from the spiritual unity which makes *The Flowers of Evil* or *Leaves of Grass* self-sufficient worlds. Darío's book is a vast repertory of rhythms, forms, colors, and sensations. It is not the history of a conscience but the metamorphosis of a sensibility. Its central theme is pleasure. But pleasure is a game, and for that very reason it is also a ritual which includes sacrifice and pain. Darío was not the first to know that the religion of pleasure is a rigorous one.

In my opinion, the last poem in *Profane Hymns* is the greatest poem in the book. It is both a résumé of his aesthetics and a prophecy about the future course of poetry. Its first line is a definition of his verse: "I seek a form that my style cannot discover." He seeks a beauty that is beyond beauty, that words can evoke but can never state. All of Romanticism—the desire to grasp the infinite—and all of Symbolism—an ideal, indefinable beauty that can only be suggested—are contained in that line. In the sestet there is an abrupt change of tone. After hope and confidence, doubt: "And I only find the word that runs away." The feeling of sterility and impotence appears as constantly in Darío's poetry as it does in that of the other great poets of the epoch, from Baudelaire to Mallarmé. At times it resolves into irony; at other times, into silence. In the concluding line, the poet sees the world as an immense question mark. It is not man who questions existence; it is existence that questions man. The line is worth the whole poem, and the poem is worth the whole book: "And the neck of the great white swan, that questions me."

In 1898 Darío became a correspondent for the Buenos Aires newspaper *La Nación*. He sailed for Europe and lived there until 1914, only returning to his homeland to die. It was a wandering life, with Paris and Mallorca its main centers. Reportorial work, diplomatic duties. Travels in Europe and the Americas. Fame and notoriety. Creation and sterility, physical and mental excesses. Empty nights, examining his conscience in a hotel room: "Why does my soul tremble so?" Finally he met Francisca Sánchez, a woman of humble origins. It was not a grand passion, but they were lovingly devoted to each other. During this epoch he published many books in prose and his great volumes of poetry: *Songs of Life and Hope, The Swans and Other Poems, The Wandering Song, Poem of Autumn and Other Poems,* and *Song to the Argentine and Other Poems.* A good many of the poems are in his previous manner; in fact, some of them were written during the time of *Profane Hymns* or even earlier. But the larger and more valuable portion reveals a new Darío, graver and more lucid, stronger and more virile. This does not imply a major break between *Profane Hymns* and *Songs of Life and Hope.* New themes appear, and the verse is more masterly and more profound, but there is no diminishing of his love for brilliant words. There is also no lack of rhythmic innovations: on the contrary, the rhythms are even more daring, and at the same time more secure. *Songs of Life and Hope* is not a negation of his earlier style but rather a natural development of it.

Among the new themes: history, both as a living tradition and as a struggle. The Spanish Americans, divided by the harsh facts of geography and the political regimes in power, were isolated not only from the rest of the world but also from their own past. Darío's generation was the first to recognize this situation, and many of the Modernists wrote impassioned defenses of their culture and equally impassioned denunciations of imperialism. During that period the United States, on the verge of becoming a world power, was extending and consolidating its domination of Latin America, using every means from Pan-American diplomacy to the "big stick." Politics always bored Darío, but he felt that he had to speak out. His opposition to imperialism was not based on a radical political theory. He never saw the United States as the embodiment of capitalism, nor the drama of Spanish America as a clash between economic and social interests; he never wavered in his admiration for Poe, for Whitman, for Emerson. What he refused to accept was the idea that Anglo-American culture was superior to Spanish-American culture. In his poem "To Roosevelt" he opposed the optimistic doctrine of Progress with a reality that was not on a material plane: the Spanish-American soul.

Although Darío found rationalist atheism repugnant—his temperament was religious, even superstitious—it cannot be said that he was a Christian poet. Fear of death, the horror of being, self-disgust, expressions which appear now and then after *Songs of Life and Hope*, are ideas and feelings with Christian roots; but the other half, Christian eschatology, is absent. Darío was born in a Christian world, but he lost his faith and was left, like so many of us, with the inheritance of a guilt that no longer has reference to a supernatural sphere. The sense of original sin impregnates many of his best poems: ignorance of our origins and our end, fear of the inner abyss, the horror of living in the dark. Nervous fatigue, made worse by disorderly living and alcoholic excesses, together with his constant coming and going from one country to another, added to his uneasiness. He would wander aimlessly, driven by his anxieties; or he would sink into lethargies that were "brutal nightmares" and in which death seemed alternately a bottomless well or a glorious awakening. In the poems of this nature, written in a temperate and reticent language, varying between monologue and confession, I am especially moved by all three of the nocturnes. The first and third conclude with a presentiment of death. He does not describe death and only names it with a pronoun: She.[2] In contrast, he sees life as a bad dream, a motley collection of grotesque or terrible moments, futile actions, un-

[2] In Spanish, "death" *(la muerte)* is a feminine noun. *(Tr.)*

realized projects, flawed emotions. It is the anguish of a city night, its silence broken by "the rumble of distant wheels" or the humming of the blood: a prayer that becomes a blasphemy, the endless reckoning of a solitary as he faces the blank wall that closes off the future. But all would resolve into a serene happiness if She would appear. Darío's eroticism never ceased, and he even made a marriage of dying.

In "Poem of Autumn," one of his last and greatest works, the two streams that feed his poetry are united: meditation on death and pantheistic eroticism. The poem is a set of variations on the old, worn-out themes of the brevity of life, the necessity of seizing the moment, and the like, but at the close the tone becomes graver and more defiant: in the face of death the poet does not affirm his own life but that of the universe. Earth and the sun vibrate in his skull as if it were a seashell; the salt of the sea is mingled in his blood as it is in that of the tritons and nereids; to die is to live a vaster, mightier life. Did he really believe this? It is true that he feared death; it is also true that he loved and desired it. Death was his Medusa and his siren. Dual death, dual like everything he touched, saw, and sang: his unity is always dual. That is why, as Juan Ramón Jiménez said, his emblem is the whorled seashell, both silent and filled with murmurs, an infinity that fits in one's hand. A musical instrument, speaking in an "unknown voice." A talisman, because "Europa touched it with her sacred hands." An erotic amulet, a ritual object. Its hoarse voice announces the dawn and the twilight, the hours when light and darkness meet. It is a symbol of universal correspondency, and also of reminiscence: when he presses it to his ear he hears the surge of past lives. He walks along the beach, where "the crabs are marking the sand with the illegible scrawl of their claws," and finds a seashell: then "a star like that of Venus" glows in his soul. The seashell is his body and his poetry, the rhythmic fluctuations, the spiral of those images that reveal and hide the world, that speak it and fall silent.

In 1914, with Europe at war, Darío returned to his native land. In addition to his physical and spiritual ailments, he was now suffering from financial difficulties. He conceived the idea of making a lecture tour throughout the continent, assisted by a fellow countryman who was to serve as his business manager. He fell sick in New York and his companion deserted him. He went back to Nicaragua, mortally ill, and died there on the 6th of February, 1916. "The seashell I found is in the shape of a heart." It was both his living breast and his dead skull.

CONTENTS

SECTION ONE

from *Abrojos* (*Thistles*)

I

First, a look;
then the burning touch
of hands; and then
the racing blood
and the kiss that triumphs.
Later, night and delight. Later, the flight
of that craven gossip
seeking another victim.
You are right to weep, but it is too late!
Do you see? I told you!

II

She wept in my arms. She was dressed all in black.
I heard the pounding, pounding of her heart.
Her chestnut-colored hair was long and fragrant,
and her whole body shivered with fear and love.
Who was to blame? The silence of the night.
I meant to leave, but when I said, "Goodbye,"
there beneath the flowering almond tree,
she sighed and clasped me fiercely to her breast.
The white clouds were guarding the white full moon.
Later, both of us wept, sadly, bitterly—

III

Are you weeping? I understand.
This is the end of it.
But oh, my dear, how it hurts
to see your tears.
Our love is forever and ever.
Our marriage—never.
Who is the bandit
that came to steal
your crown of flowers
and your wedding veil?
But no, don't tell me,
I don't want to hear it.

Your name is Innocence,
his name is Satan.
An abyss at your feet,
an insolent hand
to push you: and you fall,
while your guardian angel
turns away to weep,
disconsolate and lonely.
But why are you shedding
so many tears? Ah, yes,
I understand everything—
No, don't say any more.

IV

When the serpent whistled
and the hawk sang songs,
when the flowers groaned
and a planet sighed,
when the diamond sparkled
and the coral bled,
when Satan's eyes
were silver dollars,
that was when
she lost her virginity.

V

That childless lady despises
her own exquisite figure
when the cook comes by in the street with her six
children and a seventh on the way.

VI

What an extraordinary thing!
That very learnèd young man still knows
how to make the sign of the cross!

VII

Who is a light in the street
and darkness in his house?
He that finds flowers in the former,
but in the latter, thistles and tears.

VIII

"What lovely little verses!"
Don Julian told me—
and that phrase
had the fangs of a rabid dog,
the sting of a scorpion.

IX

Antonio, that good fellow,
has recently got married
and is happy with his wife,
for there is no one lovelier,
sweeter, and more faithful,
more filled with affection,
more free of duplicity,
gentler of character,
easier to seduce—

X

He was a priest, so poor
that it was dreadful to see
the gaps in his ruined shoes
and his old, worn-out cassock.
And he was almost a beggar,
but he knew how to share
a half of his loaf of bread
with those who were even poorer.
A priest so dedicated
to charitable acts
that if he had eaten breakfast
he went to bed without supper.
He was a poor little priest
who was known as Father Julian,
and the great ones of the city

treated him like a dog;
so innocent and mild,
so humble in every way
that he was a standing joke
in the houses of the rich.
One morning he was found dead,
but no one knew if his death
was caused by so much hunger
or some other form of disease.
Poor Father Julian was given
a solemn funeral service,
for which a small fortune
was spent on candles alone.
The funeral carriages bore
the most luxurious trappings;
the dead march was played
by uniformed musicians.
And the people say that when
the drums and oboes sounded,
it was as if they were mocking
the corpse of the poor priest—
and they say that the dead man laughed,
thinking of his old cassock,
but it was the kind of laughter
that almost makes you weep.

XI

You pity me, no?—
and I wish I had a rope
to string you up
from the nearest tree,
for you are a good fellow,
the salt of the earth,
with your soul full of envy
and your mouth full of drivel.

XII

I would not want to see you a mother,
my dark sweet woman.
But then, there is a canal
not far from your house,
and of course it is well known
that man is not born with the knowledge
of how to swim.

SECTION TWO

from *Rimas (Rhymes)*

I

That pallid afternoon, the sun
was setting, its round red face enclosed
  in a nimbus of golden dust.

Out on the sea a swift boat rowing,
rowing: the lover with his belovèd,
  flying to the land of dreams.

In the sunset light and the million glints
that flashed on the sea, those streaming oars
  seemed made of burnished gold.

And, in that graceful boat, still rowing,
rowing, the lover and his belovèd,
  flying to the land of dreams.

Their fate? I do not know. I remember
that after a pallid twilight, the sky
  darkened and the sea grew rough.

II

There was a monogram
on your white handkerchief,
the red monogram of a name that was not
your name, my love.
The fine batiste
rustled in your hands.
"How the blood stands out against the white!"
I said with a laugh,
and you turned pale;
you were afraid of me—
What did you see? Did you recognize
Othello's smile?

III

The blue bird of sleep
   crosses my brow:
There is spring in my heart
   and dawn in my mind.
I love the light, the turtledove's bill,
   the rose and the bellflower,
   the lips of a virgin,
   the heron's white neck.
   Oh Lord in Heaven,
      I know you love me.

The tragic black night
   falls on my spirit;
I seek the profound depths of its shadow
   to spill my tears.
I know there can be tempests in the mind,
   abysms in the soul,
   and mysterious furrows
   on pallid brows.
   Oh Lord in Heaven,
      I know you deceive me.

SECTION THREE

from *Azul (Blue)*

Springtime

(From "The Lyric Year")

Month of roses. My poems
wander through the vast forest
to gather honey and fragrance
from the half-opened flowers.
Come, my belovèd. The great
wood is our temple; a blessed
perfume of love is drifting
and wavering there. A bird flies
from tree to tree, and salutes
your brow, which is as rosy
as daybreak; and the live oaks,
tall and staunch and haughty,
rustle their tremulous green
leaves as you approach,
and form an arch with their boughs,
as though a queen were passing.
Oh, my belovèd! It is
the sweet season of spring.

Look: in your eyes, my own;
free your locks to the wind,
so that the sun may burnish
that wild, magnificent gold.
Allow me to clasp your hands,
which are rose petals and silk,
and smile at me with the moist
cool crimson of your lips.
I will recite you verses;
you will listen with delight,
and if a nightingale

should perch nearby and sing
of nymphs, roses, or stars,
you will not hear his trills:
amorous and enchanted,
you will hear only my songs,
your gaze fixed on my lips.
Oh, my belovèd! It is
the sweet season of spring.

There is a limpid stream
that surges from a cavern,
and beautiful white nymphs
bathe there, playful and naked.
They laugh to the sound of the foam,
they splash the clear water,
moistening their long locks
with crystal drops of dew,
and all know hymns of love
in the splendid Greek tongue
that Pan invented in the woods
in the great days of antiquity.
Belovèd, I will place
in my verses the fairest word
from all the phrases and lines
in the hymns of that language;
and you will speak that word,
which drips the honey of Hybla—
Oh, my belovèd! It is
the sweet season of spring.

A vibrant swarm of bees
is flying in the white sunlight
like a small gold whirlwind,
and the rainbow dragonflies
are darting above the sonorous

waters on crystalline wings.
Listen: the cicada is singing
because it loves the sun,
which filters its golden dust
through the clustering leaves.
Its breath gives us a fecund
sense of our mother earth,
with the very souls of the flowers,
the fragrance of the grasses.

See that nest. See the two
birds, the male and the female.
The female has a white breast,
the male's plumage is black.
A song swells their throats,
their soft wings are trembling,
and their beaks, meeting, are like
two pairs of lips kissing.
The nest is a canticle. Birds
incubate music, oh poets!
Birds vibrate one string
of the universal lyre.
Blessèd be the sacred warmth
that caused the eggs to hatch,
oh, my belovèd, in this
the sweet season of spring.

My sweet muse Delicia
brought me a Greek amphora
carved out of alabaster
and filled with Naxos wine;
and a lovely golden cup,
the base studded with pearls,
so that I might drink the wine
appropriate to poets.

Diana is on the amphora,
regally proud and tall,
with her divine nakedness
and her stance of a huntress.
And the Cytherean Venus
is on the luminous cup,
reclining beside Adonis,
who scorns her fond caresses.
But I do not want the wine
of Naxos, nor the fine amphora,
nor the cup where the Cyprian
pleads with that elegant youth.
No, I want to drink love
only from your red mouth,
oh, my belovèd, in this
the sweet season of spring!

In Winter

In these long, slow winter hours my Carolina
sits by the fire that glimmers in the salon,
curled up or half curled up in the softest chair,
enveloped in her enormous sable coat.

The white angora stretches out beside her,
rubbing his nose against the lace of her skirt;
behind them, the porcelain jardinieres from China
loom up against the Japanese silk screen.

Carolina is drugged with the sly philters of sleep.
I enter without a word, take off my gray coat,
and kiss her face, which is as rosy and bright

as a red rose that once was a fleur-de-lis.
She opens her eyes and looks at me with a smile.
Outside, the snow is still falling over Paris.

SECTION FOUR

from *Prosas profanas y otros poemas*
(Profane Hymns and Other Poems)

It Was a Gentle Air . . .

It was a gentle air, with turns and pauses;
the sprite Harmony guided all its flights;
and there were whispered words and tenuous sighs
among the sobbings of the violoncellos.

Along the terrace, next to the crowded leaves,
there was a tremolo as of aeolian harps
whenever the silken gowns, in passing, stroked
the white magnolias erect upon their stems.

The Marchioness Eulalia bestowed
her smiles and snubs on two rivals at once:
the blond viscount with his challenges,
the young *abbé* with his madrigals.

Near them, beneath a coronet of grape leaves,
bearded Terminus laughed behind his mask,
and like an ephebe that might have been a girl,
the huntress Diana revealed her naked marble.

The Mercury of Jean de Boulogne was flying
beneath a leafy bower, palestra of love,
on a sumptuous pedestal in the Ionic style;
there was a lighted torch in his right hand.

The orchestra strung its magic notes like pearls;
we heard a chorus of clear and wingèd sounds;
the sweet violins of Hungary sang out
both slow pavannes and volatile gavottes.

On hearing how her two gallants complain,
divine Eulalia laughs and laughs and laughs,
because her treasures are the arrows of Eros,
the Cyprian's girdle, and Omphale's distaff.

Alas for the man who hears her honeyed words!
Alas for the man who believes her songs of love!
With her shining eyes and curving crimson mouth
divine Eulalia laughs and laughs and laughs.

Her eyes are blue, she is lovely and perverse,
and her glances shed a strange and living light:
the soul of the crystal paleness of champagne
looks out of her pupils, which are moist and starry.

It is a festive night, and the dress ball
shows off the glory of its mundane triumphs.
Divine Eulalia, radiant in her lace,
destroys a flower with her dainty fingers.

Ah! that amorous bird who breathes pure song
and hides her bill at times beneath her wing;
who trills her insults from beneath her wing,
the soft and guileful wing of her wide fan.

And when, at midnight, Philomel pours out
her timeless grief in arpeggios of golden notes,
and the white swan, like an ivory gondola, prints
its wake upon the tranquillity of the pool,

the marchioness will vanish among the leaves,
among the clustering green that hides a bower
in which she will be clasped by the arms of a page
who, being her page, will also be her poet.

But now, divine Eulalia is with her gallants,
and now, to the rhythm of an Italian air
which the musicians loose to the wandering breeze,
divine Eulalia laughs and laughs and laughs.

Was this in the reign of Louis, king of France,
a sun with a court of stars, on an azure field?
When that majestic—that imperial—rose,
Pompadour, filled the castles with perfume?

Was this when the belle plucked up her gorgeous skirt
with a nymph's fingers, to dance the minuet,
her light and lovely feet, in crimson slippers,
following all the measures of the music?

Or was it when shepherdesses, in flowering vales,
adorned their soft white lambs with silken ribbons;
when those divine Thyrses of Versailles listened
to the overtures of the gentlemen who loved them?

Was this in those good days of shepherd dukes,
of loving princesses and tender gallants,
the days when chamberlains in their livery
moved among shining smiles and pearls and flowers?

Was this in the north, perhaps, or in the south?
I do not know the age, the hour, the country;
but this I know: Eulalia is still laughing,
and her golden laugh is cruel and eternal.

Sonatina

The Princess is sad. What ails the Princess?
Nothing but sighs escape from her lips,
which have lost their smile and their strawberry red.
The Princess is pale in her golden chair,
the keys of her harpsichord gather dust,
and a flower, forgotten, droops in its vase.

The garden is bright with the peacocks' triumph,
the duenna prattles of commonplace things,
the clown pirouettes in his crimson and gold;
but the Princess is silent, her thoughts are far-off:
the Princess traces the dragonfly course
of a vague illusion in the eastern sky.

Are her thoughts of a prince of Golconda or China?
Of a prince who has halted his silver coach
to see the soft light that glows in her eyes?
Of the king of the fragrant isle of roses,
or the lord who commands the clear-shining diamonds,
or the arrogant lord of the pearls of Ormuz?

Alas, the poor Princess, whose mouth is a rose,
would be a swallow or a butterfly;
would skim on light wings, or mount to the sun
on the luminous stair of a golden sunbeam;
would greet the lilies with the verses of May,
or be lost in the wind on the thundering sea.

She is tired of the palace, the silver distaff,
the enchanted falcon, the scarlet buffoon,
the swans reflected on the azure lake.
And the flowers are sad for the flower of the court:
the jasmines of the east, the water lilies of the north,
the dahlias of the west, and the roses of the south.

The poor little Princess with the wide blue eyes
is imprisoned in her gold, imprisoned in her tulle,
in the marble cage of the royal palace,
the lofty palace that is guarded by sentries,
by a hundred Negroes with a hundred halberds,
a sleepless greyhound, and a monstrous dragon.

Oh to be a butterfly leaving its cocoon!
(The Princess is sad. The Princess is pale.)
Oh adorable vision of gold, marble, and rose!
Oh to fly to the land where there is a prince—
(The Princess is pale. The Princess is sad.)—
more brilliant than daybreak, more handsome than April!

"Hush, Princess, hush," says her fairy godmother;
"the joyous knight who adores you unseen
is riding this way on his wingèd horse,
a sword at his waist and a hawk on his wrist,
and comes from far off, having conquered Death,
to kindle your lips with a kiss of true love!"

Blazon

For the Countess of Peralta

The snow-white Olympic swan,
with beak of rose-red agate,
preens his eucharistic wing,
which he opens to the sun like a fan.

His shining neck is curved
like the arm of a lyre,
like the handle of a Greek amphora,
like the prow of a ship.

He is the swan of divine origin
whose kiss mounted through fields
of silk to the rosy peaks
of Leda's sweet hills.

White king of Castalia's fount,
his triumph illumines the Danube;
Da Vinci was his baron in Italy;
Lohengrin is his blond prince.

His whiteness is akin to linen,
to the buds of white roses,
to the diamantine white
of the fleece of an Easter lamb.

He is the poet of perfect verses,
and his lyric cloak is of ermine;
he is the magic, the regal bird
who, dying, rhymes the soul in his song.

This wingèd aristocrat displays
white lilies on a blue field;
and Pompadour, gracious and lovely,
has stroked his feathers.

He rows and rows on the lake
where dreams wait for the unhappy,
where a golden gondola waits
for the sweetheart of Louis of Bavaria.

Countess, give the swans your love,
for they are gods of an alluring land
and are made of perfume and ermine,
of white light, of silk, and of dreams.

The Swan

It was a divine hour for the human race.
Before, the Swan sang only at its death.
But when the Wagnerian Swan began to sing,
there was a new dawning, and a new life.

The song of the Swan is heard above the storms
of the human sea; its aria never ceases;
it dominates the hammering of old Thor,
and the trumpets hailing the sword of Argentir.

Oh Swan! Oh sacred bird! If once white Helen,
immortal princess of Beauty's realms, emerged
all grace from Leda's sky-blue egg, so now,

beneath the white of your wings, the new Poetry,
here in a splendor of music and light, conceives
the pure, eternal Helen who is the Ideal.

Symphony in Gray Major

The sea, like an enormous mirror,
reflects the zinc sheet of the sky,
while distant flocks of seabirds dot
the pale, burnished gray of the background.

The sun, a disc of translucent glass,
creeps to the zenith like an invalid;
the sea wind rests in the shade, its head
pillowed on its black bugle.

The waves heave their leaden bellies,
seeming to groan under the pier.
A sailor sits on a coil of rope,
smoking his pipe and thinking of the shores
of a vague, far land of mists.

That sea dog is old now. The burning rays
of the Brazilian sun have scorched his face;
the wild typhoons of the China Sea
have watched him drink his flask of gin.

The foam, bitter with iodine and saltpeter,
has long been familiar with his red nose,
his crisp curls and athlete's biceps,
his drill shirt and canvas cap.

In the midst of his tobacco smoke
he sees that distant land of mists
for which his brigantine set sail
one hot, gold afternoon.

Tropical siesta. The sea dog sleeps.
The gamut of gray has shrouded everything,
as if a soft, huge charcoal of the curved
horizon had blurred all outlines.

Tropical siesta. The old cicada
tries out its hoarse, senile guitar,
and the cricket begins a monotonous solo
on the only string of its fiddle.

Song of the Blood

Blood of Abel. The war trumpet.
Fraternal struggles; noise, horrors;
the standards wave, the grapeshot kills,
and the emperors wear purple.

Blood of Christ. The sonorous organ.
The celestial vineyard yields celestial wine;
at the sacred lip of the golden chalice
the soul drinks the wine of eternity.

Blood of the martyrs. The psaltery.
Bonfires, lions, conquering palms;
great dawns that come from the mysterious,
announced by red heralds.

Blood the hunter spills. The horn.
The fatal weapons of the murderers
are forged in the dark smithies of hell
by red furies and scarlet destinies.

Oh blood of the virgins! The lyre.
Enchantment of honeybees and butterflies.
The star of Venus looks down from the sky
on the crimson triumph of the rose-queens.

Blood the Law spills.
A muffled drum.
Blossoming of the rosebays that Death waters,
and the red comet that foretells destruction.

Blood of the suicides. A hand organ.
Fantastic boasting, choral responses
with which the glitter of Saturn is hailed
in the poorhouse and the madhouse.

The Ear of Wheat

Look at the subtle signs that the wind's fingers
are making as they shake the stalk: it bends
and straightens in a rhythmic virtue of motion.
With the golden pencil of the flower of the wheat

they trace on the blue cloth of the firmament
the immortal mystery of the divine earth
and the soul of things that bestows its sacrament
in an eternal freshness as of morning.

The face of God looks out from the peace of the fields.
A mystic incense from the flowered urns
perfumes the great altar where the blue smile triumphs.

The tree is still green and still covered with blossoms,
the lamb is grazing under its love-filled boughs,
and the Mass sleeps in the wheat-ear of gold and sunlight.

My Soul

My soul, persist in your divine idea;
all is under the sign of a supreme destiny;
keep to your way, keep on to the last sunset
along the road that leads you toward the Sphinx.

Pluck a flower in passing, and leave the thorn;
row, row in cadence on the golden river;
salute the rude plough of rude Triptolemus,
and keep on, like a god ruled by his dreams—

And keep on, like a god inspired by good fortune;
and while the rhetoric of the birds is full of your praise,
and the stars of heaven accompany you, and the boughs
of the Tree of Hope are green with spring's arrival,
dauntlessly make your way through the Forest of Evil,
without fearing serpents, and keep on, like a god—

I Seek a Form . . .

I seek a form that my style cannot discover,
a bud of thought that wants to be a rose;
it is heralded by a kiss that is placed on my lips
in the impossible embrace of the Venus de Milo.

The white peristyle is decorated with green palms;
the stars have predicted that I will see the goddess;
and the light reposes within my soul like the bird
of the moon reposing on a tranquil lake.

And I only find the word that runs away,
the melodious introduction that flows from the flute,
the ship of dreams that rows through all space,

and, under the window of my sleeping beauty,
the endless sigh from the waters of the fountain,
and the neck of the great white swan, that questions me.

SECTION FIVE

from *Cantos de vida y esperanza*
(*Songs of Life and Hope*)

The Three Kings

"I am Gaspar. I have brought frankincense,
and I have come here to say that life is good.
That God exists. That love is everything.
I know it is so because of the heavenly star."

"I am Melchior. I have brought fragrant myrrh.
Yes, God exists. He is the light of day.
The whitest flower is rooted in the mud,
and all delights are tinged with melancholy."

"I am Balthasar. I have brought gold.
I assure you, God exists. He is great and strong.
I know it is so because of the perfect star
that shines so brightly in Death's diadem."

"Gaspar, Melchior, Balthasar: be still.
Love has triumphed, and bids you to its feast.
Christ, reborn, turns chaos into light,
and on His brows He wears the Crown of Life."

Cyrano in Spain

Behold how Cyrano de Bergerac has crossed
the Pyrenees at one bound. Cyrano is in Spain.
What is the blood in Spain but wine and fire?
La Mancha's great knight embraces the great Gascon.
Where but in Spain are such lovely castles found?
Roxanas enhance the Murillos with their roses,
and the brave cadets of Gascony all know
the Toledo blade that Quevedo swung so well.
Cyrano traveled to the moon; but, before that,
the divine lunatic of Don Miguel Cervantes
went riding among the gentle stars of his dream,
his mount that supreme Pegasus, Clavileño.
And Cyrano has read the marvelous tale,
and when he utters the name of Don Quixote
he takes off his hat; Cyrano Balazote
knows that he and Quixote speak the same tongue.
The Gascon's heroic nose is thrusting forward
to sniff the golden wines of Andalusia,
and his French sword, when he draws it from the scabbard,
gleams very well in the land of the cape and sword.
Welcome, Cyrano de Bergerac! Castile
gives you her language, and your soul shines like your blade
in the sun that in Spain was not hidden during your time.
Your nose and your plume are not in a foreign land,
for this is the very country of knight errantry,
where you are the honored guest of Calderón.
María Roxana will show you that the fragrant
roses of Spain can match the roses of France,
and your elegant bearing, your incomparable smiles,
and your glances, which are stars dressed in black capes,
will win you an enchanting Spanish Roxana.

Oh, poet! Great, grotesque, celestial poet!
Brave and noble, fearless and without fault,
the prince of lunacies, of dreams and verses:
your plume is brother to the tallest peaks,
a lark flies up from the nest that is your soul,
and you have a fairy godmother, who is Despair;
while, in the wood of grief and forgetfulness,
the nine Muses bind your wounded heart.
Up there in the moon did you find a magic lawn
on which poor Pierrot wanders, a desolate ghost?
Did you see the white palace of the madmen of Art?
Did the great shade of Pindar come to meet you?
Did you glimpse the red stain on the white stones
which is the castle of the demented virgins?
And did you hear, within a fantastic garden
of mysterious flowers, the King of the Nightingales?
I beg you not to misunderstand my questions,
for all these things, and more, exist on the moon.
Welcome, Cyrano de Bergerac! Cyrano
de Bergerac, cadet and lover, and Spaniard
who brings us such memories as Durandel bestows
on the land where Tizona, sword of the Cid, still flashes.
Art is the glorious conqueror. It is Art
that conquers time and space; and oh, peoples,
its standard is the blue oriflamme of the spirit.
Who of the elect would pause if its trumpet called?
Not one; the answer comes across the centuries:
the *Song of Roland* and the *Geste* of the Cid.
Cyrano comes marching, poet and knight,
to the sounding beat of our grave, ancient ballads.
His haughty plume is surrounded by an aureole.
His fine bright spurs were fashioned here in Spain.
And Rostand, weaving the envoy of his ballade,
would seem to look at Quevedo with a challenge.
Welcome, Cyrano de Bergerac! The years

cannot wither your glory; the old Spanish theater
hails the mighty ambassador of great Molière,
and Tirso pours his wine into Gallic cups.
We crush the grapes of Champagne to drink a toast
to you and France in a glass of Spanish crystal.

Greetings to Leonardo

Master, Pomona raises her basket. Your race
salutes the dawn. Your dawn! May it wipe out
the stain of indifference, and break
the strong chain of centuries, and crush
the toad with a stone from its sling.
The Gioconda has no sweeter smile.
Verse with its wings and rhythm with its sling
become brothers in one
sweetness of the moon
gliding gently on the lake
(the rhythm of the waves and the verse of the wings
of the magic Swan on the lake).

And thus, incomparable Master
of inspiration,
the vague figures
of a dream are embodied in lines so pure
that the dream
receives the blood of the mortal world,
and Psyche attains her deep desire
to be known across the terrestrial crystal.

(The clowns
who make Mona Lisa smile
know songs
that once were sung in the woods of Greece
by the laughing breeze.)

His Eminence goes by.
Like a flower or a sin
in his red robes.
Like a flower or a sin, or the conscience
of the subtle monseigneur who glares at his page
with vague suspicion or anger.
Naples permits the golden bee
to make its honey
during its blue fiesta; and the sonorous
pandore and the laurel
announce that here is Florence.
Master, if there in Rome
the sun of Segor and Sodom burns
the bitter science
of purple banners, your face
redeems the palms for us
under the arches
of your genius: St. Mark's and Parthenon
of lights and lines and lives.

(Your clowns
who cause Mona Lisa
to smile
know your ancient songs.)

The lions of Ahaseuras
surround the throne to receive you,
while the divine Monarch smiles;
but you will find danger,
danger to your Fate,

if you leave in the lyrical ship
with your Giaconda—
The wind
and the waves
know the tempest for your cargo.

But Master,
you were skillful in taming and riding
passions and illusions:
you tamed the first with the bridle,
the second with the halter,
zebras or lions.
And in the forest of the Sun
you imprisoned the wild beast
of the light; and that mad thing was gentle
when you said, "Enough."
You steeped your Esther in aromas for six months.
The doves flew up from your royal roofs.
For your scepter and your sensitive grace,
for your golden cup, of which the roses dream,
I have in my city, which is your captive,
a garden of marble and precious stones
that is guarded by a living sphinx.

To Roosevelt

The voice that would reach you, Hunter, must speak
in Biblical tones, or in the poetry of Walt Whitman.
You are primitive and modern, simple and complex;
you are one part George Washington and one part Nimrod.
    You are the United States,
future invader of our naive America
with its Indian blood, an America
that still prays to Christ and still speaks Spanish.

You are a strong, proud model of your race;
you are cultured and able; you oppose Tolstoy.
You are an Alexander-Nebuchadnezzar,
breaking horses and murdering tigers.
(You are a Professor of Energy,
as the current lunatics say).

You think that life is a fire,
that progress is an irruption,
that the future is wherever
your bullet strikes.
                    No.

The United States is grand and powerful.
Whenever it trembles, a profound shudder
runs down the enormous backbone of the Andes.
If it shouts, the sound is like the roar of a lion.
And Hugo said to Grant: "The stars are yours."
(The dawning sun of the Agentine barely shines;
the star of Chile is rising . . .) A wealthy country,
joining the cult of Mammon to the cult of Hercules;
while Liberty, lighting the path
to easy conquest, raises her torch in New York.

But our own America, which has had poets
since the ancient times of Nezahualcóyotl;
which preserved the footprints of great Bacchus,
and learned the Panic alphabet once,
and consulted the stars; which also knew Atlantis
(whose name comes ringing down to us in Plato)
and has lived, since the earliest moments of its life,
in light, in fire, in fragrance, and in love—
the America of Moctezuma and Atahualpa,
the aromatic America of Columbus,
Catholic America, Spanish America,
the America where noble Cuauhtémoc said:
"I am not on a bed of roses"—our America,
trembling with hurricanes, trembling with Love:
O men with Saxon eyes and barbarous souls,
our America lives. And dreams. And loves.
And it is the daughter of the Sun. Be careful.
Long live Spanish America!
A thousand cubs of the Spanish lion are roaming free.
Roosevelt, you must become, by God's own will,
the deadly Rifleman and the dreadful Hunter
before you can clutch us in your iron claws.

And though you have everything, you are lacking one thing:
   God!

Towers of God! Poets!

Towers of God! Poets!
Lightning rods of Heaven
that resist the fierce storms
like solitary mountains,
like peaks in the wilderness!
Breakwaters of eternity!

Magic hope foretells
the day when the traitorous siren
will die on her musical rock.
Hope! Let us still hope!

Still hope. The bestial element
consoles itself with its hatred
of blessèd poetry, hurling
insults from race to race.

The rebellion from below
is against excellence.
The cannibal waits for his chunk of flesh
with red gums and sharpened teeth.

Towers, fasten a smile to your banner.
Confront this evil and suspicion
with a proud puff of the breeze
and the tranquillity of the sea and the sky—

Song of Hope

A great flock of crows defiles the heavenly blue.
A millenial blast of wind brings threats of pestilence.
Men are being murdered in the Far East.

Has the apocalyptic Antichrist been born?
There have been omens, there have been prodigal sights,
and it would appear the return of Christ is at hand.

The world is overwhelmed by a grief so deep
that the dreamer, that imperial philosopher,
suffers the anguish of the whole world's heart.

The hangmen of ideals afflict all lands,
humanity is trapped in a pit of shadow
with the rough curs of hatred and of war.

O Lord Jesus, why wait longer, why delay
to stretch your hand of light over the wild beasts
and let your divine banners flash in the sun?

Come to us soon and pour the essence of life
on each insane or sad or stony heart
that loves the shadows and forgets your dawn.

Come, Lord, come bringing us your glory,
come with a tremble of stars and a horror of chaos,
come bringing peace and love across the abyss.

And let your white horse, which the visionary saw,
pass by, and let the divine trumpet sound.
My heart will be a red-hot coal in your thurible.

Censer

Spes

Jesus, incomparable pardoner of wrongs,
hear me. Sower of wheat, give me the tender
bread of the Mass. Protect me from Hell's power
with the grace that washes away all wrath and lust.

Tell me that this horrible dread of agony
which possesses me is my own wicked fault;
that, dead, I will see the light of a new day,
and then will hear you say, "Arise and walk!"

Triumphal March

The procession is coming!
The procession is coming! You can hear the clear trumpets,
and the swords flash in the sun:
the procession of the paladins, gold and iron, is coming.

The solemn glory of the standards,
borne in the strong hands of heroic athletes,
is passing beneath tall arches adorned
with figures of Mars and white Minerva,
triumphal arches where Fame lifts her long bugle.
You can hear the clattering weapons of the knights,
the bold war horses champing their bits,
their hooves wounding the earth,
and the drummers
beating out the step with martial rhythms.

Thus the fierce warriors pass
beneath the triumphal arches!

The clear trumpets sound their music,
their sonorous song,
their fervent chorus,
surrounding the august pomp of the flags
with a golden thunder.
It speaks of struggle, wounded vengeance,
the rough manes of the horses,
rude crests, the pike and spear,
and blood that watered the earth
with heroic crimson;
of the black mastiffs
which death urges forward, which battle governs.

The golden sounds
announce the triumphant
arrival of Glory;
leaving the peak that guards their nests,
unfolding their enormous wings to the wind,
the condors arrive! Victory has arrived!
The procession is passing.
A grandfather points out the heroes to his grandson.
See how the old man's beard
surrounds the child's gold ringlets with its ermine.
And beautiful women are fashioning crowns of flowers,
their faces under the porticoes are roses,
and the loveliest of them
smiles at the fiercest of the warriors.
Honor to him who brings the strange banner he captured,
honor to the wounded, honor to the faithful soldiers
who were slain by alien hands.
Trumpets! Laurels!

The noble swords of the glorious past
salute the new crowns and triumphs from their panoplies:
the old swords of the grenadiers, who were stronger than bears,
the brothers of those lancers who were centaurs.
The warlike trumpets resound,
the winds are filled with voices—
Hail to those ancient swords,
those illustrious arms
that embody the glories of the past,
and hail to the sun that shines on these new-won victories,
to the hero leading his cluster of fierce young men,
to the soldier who loves the ensign of his native land,
to the soldier who, his sword in hand,
defied the sun through long red summers
and the wind and snow of cruel winters,
the night, and the frost,
and hatred, and death, immortal servant of the homeland—
the heroes are hailed by the brazen voices
that sound the triumphal march!

SECTION SIX

from *Los cisnes y otros poemas*
(*The Swans and Other Poems*)

For One Moment, Oh Swan . . .

For one moment, oh Swan, I will join my longings
with those of your two wings that once clasped Leda,
and you, in silk, will tell my maturing dreams,
through Castor and Pollux, of all the heavens' glory.

It is autumn now. The flute pours out its counsels.
For one instant, oh Swan, in the darkening grove,
I will drink with my two lips what modesty
forbids, disdaining scruples and suspicions.

Swan, for an instant your white wings will be mine,
and the roselike heart within your glorious breast
will beat within my own with your strong blood.

Love will be happy, because of the vibrant joy
that Pan will feel as he spies from his green ambush,
and the diamantine fount will hide a rhythm.

Tropical Afternoon

The afternoon is sad and gray.
The sea is dressed in velvet
and the sky is swathed in grief.

A bitter, sonorous complaint
arises from the abyss.
The waves, when the wind sings, weep.

The violins of the fog lament
for the dying day. The white foam
intones a *miserere.*

Harmony floods the sky
and the wind carries the deep
and mournful song of the sea.

Strange music bursts from the horizon's
trumpets, as if it were
the reverberating voice of the mountain—

as if it were the Invisible—
as if it were the thunder that a lion
hurls into the wind.

Nocturne

I want to express my anguish in verses that speak
of my vanished youth, a time of dreams and roses,
and the bitter defloration of my life
by many small cares and one vast aching sorrow.

And the voyage to a dim orient in half-seen ships,
the seeds of prayer that flowered in blasphemies,
the bewilderment of a swan among the puddles,
the false nocturnal blue of a sick Bohemia.

Far-off harpsichord, silent and forgotten,
that never gave my dreams the sublime sonata;
orphan skiff, heraldic tree, dark nest
which the night made lovely with its silver light—

Hope still aromatic with fresh herbs; the trill
of the nightingale in the morning in the spring;
the white lily cut down by a fatal destiny;
the search for happiness, and evil's persecutions—

And the dismal amphora with its divine poison
that causes the inner torments of this life;
the fearful knowledge of our human mire;
and the horror of knowing that we are transitory,

the horror of walking blindly, among alarms,
toward the unknowable, toward the inevitable;
and the brute nightmares that rack our weeping sleep,
from which no one but She can wake us up!

Philosophy

Come, spider, greet the sun and be of good will.
Come, toad, give thanks to God that you exist.
The shaggy crabs, like roses, all have thorns,
and the mollusks, reminiscences of women.

Learn to be what you are, embodied enigmas,
and leave the responsibility to the Norms,
who pass it on in turn to the All-Powerful—
(Come, cricket, sing in the moonlight; bear, come dance.)

Leda

The swan in shadow seems to be of snow;
his beak is translucent amber in the daybreak;
gently that first and fleeting glow of crimson
tinges his gleaming wings with rosy light.

And then, on the azure waters of the lake,
when dawn has lost its colors, then the swan,
his wings outspread, his neck a noble arc,
is turned to burnished silver by the sun.

The bird from Olympus, wounded by love, swells out
his silken plumage, and clasping her in his wings
he ravages Leda there in the singing water,
his beak seeking the flower of her lips.

She struggles, naked and lovely, and is vanquished,
and while her cries turn sighs and die away,
the screen of teeming foliage parts and the wild
green eyes of Pan stare out, wide with surprise.

Pity for Him Who One Day . . .

Pity for him who one day looks upon
his inward sphinx and questions it. He is lost.
And pity for him who pleads to joy or sorrow.
There are two gods, who are Ignorance and Forgetfulness.

We crystallize, in words and thoughts, what the tree
would like to say and what it says to the wind,
and what the animal manifests with its instincts.
But the only difference lies in the way of speaking.

In the Land of Allegory

In the Land of Allegory
Salome dances forever
before King Herod on his throne.
And the head of John the Baptist,
who caused lions to tremble,
falls to the axe. Blood rains down.
But the sexual rose, as it opens,
affects all that exists
with its carnal effluvium
and its spiritual enigma.

Melancholy

Brother, you that have light, please give me light.
I am like a blind man. I grope about in the dark.
I am lost among tempests, lost among torments, blinded
by fantasies, and driven mad by music.

That is my curse. To dream. For poetry
is an iron vest with a thousand cruel spikes
that I wear around my soul. The bloody points
let fall the endless drops of my melancholy.

I wander blind and mad through this bitter world;
at times, I think the way is very long,
and, at times, very short—

And, in this wavering between courage and agony,
I bear a load of grief I can scarcely support.
Can you hear the drops of my melancholy falling?

Alleluya

Roses, rose-red and white, and green
boughs and bright corollas and fresh
bouquets. Happiness!

Nests in the warm trees,
eggs in the warm nests,
devotion. Happiness!

The kiss of this blonde girl,
and of this tawny girl,
and of this black girl. Happiness!

And the smooth belly of the girl
who is only fifteen and the harmony
of her arms. Happiness!

And the breath of the virgin forest,
of the virgin women,
and the sweet rhymes of daybreak.
Happiness, happiness, happiness!

In Autumn

I know there are those who ask: Why does he not
sing with the same wild harmonies as before?
But they have not seen the labors of an hour,
the work of a minute, the prodigies of a year.

I am an agèd tree that, when I was growing,
uttered a vague, sweet sound when the breeze caressed me.
The time for youthful smiles has now passed by:
now, let the hurricane swirl my heart to song!

The Seashell

I found a golden seashell on the beach.
It is massive, and embroidered with the finest pearls.
Europa touched it with her sacred hands
as she rode the waves astride the celestial bull.

I raised that sounding seashell to my lips
to rouse the echoes of the ocean's reveilles,
and pressed it to my ear and heard the blue
fathoms whisper the secret of their treasures.

Hence I have tasted the salt of the bitter winds
that swelled the sails of the Argonauts when all
the stars were in love with Jason's golden dream,

and I hear a murmur of waves and an unknown voice
and a vast tide-swell and a mysterious wind—
(The shell I found is in the shape of a heart.)

Autumn Sonnet to the Marquis of Bradomin

Marquis (so like the Divine), I send you greetings.
It is autumn, and I have come back from a sad Versailles.
It was very cold, and the people wandering there
were all so coarse, and Verlaine's fountain was mute.

I stopped to brood before a naked marble,
when suddenly I saw a dove go flying past,
and by some quirk of unconscious cerebration
I thought at once of you. I do not know why.

Versailles in the autumn; a passing dove; a lovely
statue; and an aimless, vulgar city crowd;
my constant pleasure in your subtle prose;

the latest word of your triumphs— I have no other
way of explaining why these things have moved me
to send you this bouquet of autumn roses.

Nocturne

You that have heard the heartbeat of the night,
you that have heard, in the long, sleepless hours,
a closing door, the rumble of distant wheels,
a vague echo, a wandering sound from somewhere:

you, in the moments of mysterious silence,
when the forgotten ones issue from their prison—
in the hour of the dead, in the hour of repose—
will know how to read the bitterness in my verses.

I fill them, as one would fill a glass, with all
my grief for remote memories and black misfortunes,
the nostalgia of my flower-intoxicated soul
and the pain of a heart grown sorrowful with fêtes;

with the burden of not being what I might have been,
the loss of the kingdom that was awaiting me,
the thought of the instant when I might not have been born
and the dream my life has been ever since I was!

All this has come in the midst of that boundless silence
in which the night develops earthly illusions,
and I feel as if an echo of the world's heart
had penetrated and disturbed my own.

Thanatos

Nel mezzo del camin di nostra vita—
so Dante said. But it has been changed:
In the middle of the thoroughfare to Death.

And there is no reason to hate
the queen—the empress—of Nothing.
She weaves the fabric of our lives,
and pours into the cup of dreams
an opposite nepenthe—she never forgets!

Far Away

Ox that I saw in my childhood, as you steamed
in the burning gold of the Nicaraguan sun,
there on the rich plantation filled with tropical
harmonies; woodland dove, of the woods that sang
with the sound of the wind, of axes, of birds and wild bulls:
I salute you both, because you are both my life.

You, heavy ox, evoke the gentle dawn
that signaled it was time to milk the cow,
when my existence was all white and rose;
and you, sweet mountain dove, cooing and calling,
you signify all that my own springtime, now
so far away, possessed of the Divine Springtime.

Fatality

The tree is happy because it is scarcely sentient;
the hard rock is happier still, it feels nothing:
there is no pain as great as being alive,
no burden heavier than that of conscious life.

To be, and to know nothing, and to lack a way,
and the dread of having been, and future terrors . . .
And the sure terror of being dead tomorrow,
and to suffer all through life and through the darkness,

and through what we do not know and hardly suspect . . .
And the flesh that tempts us with bunches of cool grapes,
and the tomb that awaits us with its funeral sprays,
and not to know where we go,
nor whence we came! . . .

SECTION SEVEN

from *El canto errante (The Wandering Song)*

Metempsychosis

I was a soldier who slept in the bed
of Cleopatra the Queen. Her whiteness,
her starlike, omnipotent gaze.
      That was all.

Oh her gaze, her whiteness, and the bed
in which her whiteness was so radiant!
Oh marble and omnipotent rose!
      That was all.

And her spine creaked in my arms;
and I, a freedman, made her forget Antony.
(Oh her bed, her gaze, her whiteness!)
      That was all.

I, Rufus Gallus, was a soldier, my blood
was Gallic, and the imperial calf
gave me a daring moment of her caprices.
      That was all.

Why, in our spasm, did the pincers
of my bronze fingers not squeeze the throat
of that white queen as a jest?
      That was all.

I was taken to Egypt, with a chain
around my neck. One day I was eaten
by the dogs. My name, Rufus Gallus.
      That was all.

To Columbus

Unfortunate admiral! Your poor America,
your beautiful, hot-bloooded, virgin Indian love,
the pearl of your dreams, is now hysterical,
her nerves convulsing and her forehead pale.

A most disastrous spirit rules your land:
where once the tribesmen raised their clubs together,
now there is endless warfare between brothers,
the selfsame races wound and destroy each other.

The stone idol is gone, and in its place
a living idol sits upon a throne,
while every day the pallid dawn reveals
the blood and ashes in the fields of neighbors.

Disdaining kings, we give ourselves our laws
to the sound of cannons and of bugle-calls,
and now, on the sinister behalf of black kings,
each Judas is a friend of every Cain.

We love to drink the festive wines of France;
day after day we sing the *Marseillaise*
in our indigenous, semi-Spanish voices,
but end by roaring out the *Carmagnole*.

The treacheries of ambition never cease,
the dream of freedom lies in broken bits.
This crime was never committed by our chiefs,
by those to whom the mountains gave their arrows.

They were majestic, loyal, and great-hearted;
their heads were decorated with rare feathers.
Oh if the white men who came had only been
like the Atahualpas and the Moctezumãs!

When once the seed of the iron race from Spain
was planted in the womb of the Americas,
the heroic strength of great Castile was mixed
with the strength of our own Indians of the mountains.

Would to God that these waters, once untouched,
had never mirrored the white of Spanish sails,
and that the astonished stars had never seen
those caravels arriving at our shores!

The mountains saw how the natives, who were free
as eagles, came and went in the wild forest,
hunting the deer, the puma, and the bison
with the sure arrows they carried in their quivers.

A chief, though rough and bizarre, is worth far more
than a soldier who roots his glory in the mud,
who has caused the brave to groan beneath his car
or the frozen mummies of Incan lords to tremble.

The cross you brought to us is now decayed,
and after the revolution of the rabble,
the rabble writing today defiles the language
written by great Cervantes and Calderón.

A gaunt and feeble Christ walks through the streets,
Barabbas can boast of slaves and epaulets,
and the lands of Chibcha, Cuzco, and Palenque
have seen wild beasts acclaimed and decorated.

Evil mischance has placed afflictions, horrors,
wars, and unending fevers in our way:
Oh Christopher Columbus, unfortunate admiral,
pray to God for the world that you discovered!

1892

Revelation

From the brink of a cliff above the sea
I hurled a cry that filled
my mouth with the wind and the brine:

a cry to the blue vistas of infinity,
the magnificent, bleeding west,
the crimson sun, all miracle and myth.

And I thought I tasted in the wind and brine
a communion of communions
that wounded my thoughts and senses.

The lives of palpitating hearts,
the light that science devises in its entrails,
and the prodigy of the constellations.

And I heard the voice of the god of the mountains
who announced his return
with the marvelous notes of his seven reeds.

And I cried: "It is true, the great god
of force and life, the great god Pan,
is immortal, he has never died!"

And I saw how that strange double serpent,
entwined about the celestial caduceus,
suddenly crossed the waves,

borne in the hands of Mercury. And my thoughts
turned my eyes to mother Thalassa,
for when I look at the sea I find everything.

And I saw blue and topaz and amethyst,
gold and pearl, silver and violet,
and the conquest of Electra's daughter.

And I heard the hoarse trumpet-blasts
that Triton sounds on his conch-shell,
and the song of the siren, the poet's love.

And then, in the voice of one who aspires and loves,
I cried: "Where is the god who causes
the wheat to rise from the mud, the wheat

that saves the ideal outcasts in their exodus?"
And I heard an inner voice: "I am with you,
I am in you and of you: I am the All."

Tutecotzumí

When it digs into the soil of the ancient city,
the metal tip of my poet's pick turns up
a golden brooch, a fragment of sculptured stone,
an arrow, a fetish, a strange, ambiguous god,
or the vast walls of a temple. My pick is working
deep in the soil of this unknown America,
turning up gold and opals and precious stones,
an altar, a broken statue. And the Muse
divines the meaning of the hieroglyphics.

The strange life of a vanished people emerges
from the mists of time; old legends, once obscure,
are clear; the mountain where the ruins lie
divulges secrets. The ancient trees have seen
processions, battles, immemorial rites.
A mockingbird is singing. What is it singing?
A song that no one has ever heard before?
The mockingbird has nested in an idol's niche.

(The Toltec women listened to that song,
and it delighted the great lord Moctezuma.)
And while the panther rustles the dry leaves,
the green quetzal shows off its glorious plumage
and the gods enliven the accents of the fountain.
At the end of the afternoon, the bloody west
spreads out its barbarous cloak, and the vague winds
carry the musical speech of some rare lyre.

And Nezahualcóyotl, king and poet, sighs.

Cuaucmichín, the noble chief and priest,
returns from the hunt, behind him a double file
of archers. His air is haughty and triumphant.
He wears a circlet of burnished gold on his brow,
and the sun, climbing above the trees, reveals
the quetzal feather that quivers in its front.

It is a magic morning in the burning tropics.
The swollen river flows like a great serpent,
with dry leaves drifting down its greenish waters.
It is a gleaming canvas, wrinkled at times
by the crooked shell the tortoise hauls about
or the alligator's crested iron tail.

Next to the still, green pool, above the rough stones,
ruby, crystal, sapphire, the flies, humming,
sift through the tulle of the vapor from the ground;
and the blue butterfly, who is all attired
in a rich velvet, fans the muddy soil,
as if in ecstasy, with his duplicate fan.

The frowning forest vibrates with the day's heat,
the black turkey raises his raucous cry,
and the cricket sings in the tall, close-standing reeds;
a wood bird imitates the sound of a horn,
the cicada keeps up its everlasting racket,
and the woodpecker repeats his shrieking whistle.

The squirrel climbs the avocado tree;
his tail is a plume, his little eyes are bright
as he bites into the ripe and luscious fruit;
and the trumpeter magpie, that dark rogue and vagrant
whose flight frightens the wasp, goes winging by,
signaling to his companion with peevish cries.

The ancient groves exhale their giant breath,
the shy quetzals fly at the slightest sound,
the hummingbird is hovering over the birthwort;
and the iguana, perched beside a sumptuous orchid,
is like a mysterious daughter of the Indian mountain,
inspired by the hidden god of the sacred temple.

Great Cuaucmichín has left the emerald woods.
He strides to his palace, his quiver at his back,
a gilded quiver that glitters in the sunlight.
Behind him go his archers, while his servants
bear on their shoulders the bleeding mountain stags
that fell to the limber arrows of the hunters.

Great Cuauchmichín arrives at his stately palace.
He sees the bright huipil of his lovely daughter,
Otzotzkij, in the oaken frame of the doorway.
Suddenly there is the rumble of a deep voice.
Is that the Montagua, and is it flooding the city?
No, chieftain: that is the anger of the Pipiles.

Like a human torrent, rising and overflowing,
with a dreadful roar that deafens the whole city,
the children of Ahuitzol are coming to the palace.
First, the high priests, the nobles and dignitaries,
adorned with gleaming feathers of a hundred kinds,
all proudly wearing their many-colored cloaks;

behind them, rank on rank, the brawny warriors
bearing their weapons, bearing their leather shields,
the soldiers of Sakulen, the soldiers of Nebaj;

and last, the wild Ixiles from the mountains,
copper-colored, savage, armed with bows and arrows,
their naked bodies red with strange tattooing.

They surround the palace as a river surrounds a rock.
Their angry shouting reaches to the heavens,
great as the voice of the mountain, the voice of the storm.
There are tall youths of fierce and noble mien,
old men who understand the ways of magic,
warlocks who dare invoke great Tamagastad.

And they are led by Tekij, inspired, majestic,
famed for his courage, famed for his sacred poems,
with the light of visions glowing in his eyes.
His golden neckpiece is a feathered serpent,
his stout sandals are made from the hide of a bull,
and he holds his brow aloft like a young lion.

The chieftain stands erect in the door of his palace.
Tekij holds up both hands, and this, like a dike,
restrains the surging torrent of sound and motion.
Cuaucmichín insolently leans on his supple bow;
his lips are twisted into a contemptuous smile
and his black eyebrows form an angry arc:

an arc from which he shoots a look like an arrow
over the thousand heads of the clamoring throng;
an arc like the dreaded bow of Hurakán.
Then Tekij speaks to the prince, who listen coldly,
and his great words, as they pierce the sweltering air,
are like the divine thunder of a Titan's wrath.

"Cuaucmichín, the mountain speaks to you in my voice.
The earth is angry, the Pipiles are in tears,
and your totem, the serpent-opossum, is a curse.
You are a cowardly beast among innocent cattle.
Why have you shed the blood of the Pipiles
like a mountain lion, Cuaucmichín, Cuaucmichín?

"Cuaucmichín! The eighth king of the Mexicans
was a great king. If he signaled with his hand,
more than a million arrows darkened the sun.
His throne was of solid gold, as was his counsel.
He cherished the sages, begged advice of the elders,
his mace was heavy. His name was Ahuitzol.

"Quelenes, Zapotecas, Tendales, Katchikeles,
the Mames who adorn themselves with opals and hides,
the war-hardened chieftains of the fierce Kiché,
all feared the power of that great Mexican king,
who, as the gods themselves do, held in his hand
the arrow that is the lightning in the storm.

"He wished to reign in peace and build his kingdom.
This was just. And there were rich virgin lands
in Guatemala, and mountains to populate.
Ahuitzol sent five men to conquer the region,
without shields or lances, bows or quivers,
without an army or show of martial pomp.

"The five men were Pipiles: they were our fathers,
and they were builders and reapers, skilled in all
the practices of peace; they planted indigo,
made lime for mortar, traded hides and birds;
and thus those rustic, gentle, glorious men
laid down the great foundations of our people.

"Pipil means child: that is, frank and ingenuous.
An old man with white hair came among them,
and everyone regarded him as a king.
Then came a handsome youth who breached the mountain,
shot his unerring arrows at the eagles,
and sang his joyous song in the midst of tempests.

"The king died; death is the ruler of kings.
Our fathers formulated our sacred laws,
and spoke with their gods in the language of the truth.

One day, in the forest, Votán told an old man
that he never drank the blood of human sacrifice,
that blood is crimson *chicha* for Tamagastad.

"For that reason, we Pipiles never offer it;
we gather the fragrant fruit of the plantain tree
to offer it to our blest and faithful god.
The ritual knife spills only blood of beasts:
but yesterday, oh infamous Cuaucmichín,
in a cruel slaughter you offered blood of Pipiles."

"I am the warrior-chief, the warrior-priest!"
the chieftain roared. Tekij called to the crowd:
"He shows the claws of a tiger, so a tiger he is!"
And like a lull in a storm, the outcry rising
above those angry heads, those shaken fists,
was still for a moment, only to rage again.

"Bowmen, to battle!" the furious chief commanded,
but it was as if he now did not exist:
the bowmen stood immobile, silent, waiting.
"Bowmen, death to the tiger!" a warrior cried.
Tekij held up his arms once more, and so
the ready arrows were not loosed from the bows.

And Tekij cried: "He is unworthy of our arrows!
The earth is trembling in its desire for vengeance!
Stone him, Pipiles!"
                    When the fierce shouts
of the crowd had ceased at last, and the hated chieftain
lay a demolished thing in the blood-red mud,
a man came by who sang a Mexican song
in a mighty voice. He sang of heaven and earth,
he praised the gods and cursed the plague of war.
They hailed him: "You sing of work and peace?" "I do."
"Then take your palace and fields, your arms, your people.
Honor our gods and govern the Pipiles."

Thus began the reign of Tutecotzumí.

Vision

I saw a sculptured mountain
rise to the skies
behind the mysterious forest,

its base in shadow.
And that mountain was the home
of the thunder, the lightning, and the wind.

A lion roared
among its black arches. And that dark
cathedral to an unknown god,

that fabulous architecture
built of prodigies and visions—
that monumental vision—terrified me.

Lions roamed at its foot,
and its towers and golden arrows
mingled with the stars.

And there was a vast, diamantine dome
where a strange throne was raised
on a sea-blue ground.

It was iron and stone below, then Parian
marble, with magic metals above.
A staircase led to the sanctuary

of the divine see. The splendor
of the starlight bathed
the triple stairs, and colossal

eagles, their wings outstretched,
were circling in the center
of an atmosphere of lights and lives.

And a white dove soared
in the pale gold of the moonlight,
a wingèd pearl in a mystic lake.

The sculptured mountain seemed
a tremendous Tower of Babel
designed by Piranesi, and on its flanks

the rock seemed to have been carved
by the lightning, while above, a vast
frieze received a golden kiss from the light,

the light of dawn and paradise.
And I cried out in the shadows: "Where
is my soul wandering now?" And suddenly

Estela, who so often enters my songs,
appeared beside me, garlanded with white
roses and orange blossoms,

telling me, in the voice of Philomel:
"Do not fear. This is the kingdom
of Dante's lyre, and the dove that flies

in the light is Beatrice. Supreme love
and the highest desire are united here.
Those who adore and who marvel come here."

"And what is that throne?" I asked.
"The throne on which the Ghibelline Orpheus
sits in glory, crowned with laurel.

And the tempest sleeps below it.
And the eyes of the wolf and the lion
shine in the darkness like coals.

And that vast, mysterious wall
is stone and iron; the arches above it
are of marble; and then, above them,

all is pure gold, and there the sacrosanct Rose
of Roses opens to the infinite
in glorious and eternal dawns."

"Oh blessèd is God!" I cried,
"who allowed the archangel of Florence
to leave us a world of mystery written

in human words with superhuman wisdom;
to fashion this strange, eternal empire
and that radiant throne on its heights,

before which I prostrate myself.
How fortunate the man who rises to Heaven
on the iron stairs of his Hell!"

And she said: "Then let your voice
sing of this wonder." And I: "Through human love
I have reached the divine. Glory to Dante!"

She raised her gracious hand to show me
the wheeling of the eagles,
and then she rose like a sovereign lily

toward Beatrice, the dove of the heavens.
And she left white footprints on the blue
that were both my joy and my consolation.

And I saw that the stars were looking at me!

Evening

Peace, peace— And now the golden city
has entered into the mysteries of evening.
The cathedral is a great reliquary.
The bay unites its crystals
in a blue like that of the archaic letters
in antiphonals and missals.
The fishing boats display the white
of their triangular sails,
and the blended aroma of salt and flowers
is like an echo that says: "Ulysses."

Eheu!

Here, beside the Latin sea,
I speak the truth:
I sense my antiquity
in the rocks, the oil, the wine.

How ancient I am, dear God,
how ancient I am!
Where has my song come from?
And where am I going?

The cost of knowing my own self
is long moments
of the most profound despair
and the how and the when—

And this Latin clarity,
what use is it here
at the entrance to the mine
of the me and the not-me?

I am a student of the clouds,
I think I can interpret
the confidences of the wind,
the earth and the sea—

A few vague confidences
about being and non-being,
and fragments of awareness
from today and yesterday.

I stopped and cried out,
as if in the midst of a desert,
and I thought the sun was dead,
and I burst into tears.

Slings

I dreamt that I was a Mallorcan slinger.
I hunted wolves, and eagles in flight,
with the stones I gathered on the beach,
and when there was war, I warred
against a thousand of the enemy.

A pebble of solid gold flew up
to the zenith one afternoon
when I saw an enormous gerfalcon
in the blue heights, pursuing

a strange and radiant bird, a ruby
that streaked the sky with sapphire.

My stone never fell back to earth.
But that cherubim-bird
came down to me at once.
"It broke out from Goliath's wound,"
the bird said, "and I have come to you.
I am David's luminous soul!"

Nocturne

Silence of the night, a sad, nocturnal
silence— Why does my soul tremble so?
I hear the humming of my blood,
and a soft storm passes through my brain.
Insomnia! Not to be able to sleep, and yet
to dream. I am the autospecimen
of spiritual dissection, the auto-Hamlet!
To dilute my sadness
in the wine of the night
in the marvelous crystal of the dark—
And I ask myself: When will the dawn come?
Someone has closed a door—
Someone has walked past—
The clock has rung three— If only it were She!—

Agency

The news?— The earth trembles.
They are hatching war in The Hague.
The crowned heads are all frightened.
The whole world smells rotten.
There is no balm in Gilead.
The Marquis de Sade has landed,
just in from Seboim.
The Gulf Stream has changed course.
Paris whips itself to delight.
They say a comet is approaching.
The predictions of that old monk
Malachi are coming true.
The Devil is hiding in the church.
A nun gave birth— (but where?—)
Barcelona is nothing now
except when a bomb explodes.
China has cut off its pigtail.
Henry de Rothschild is a poet.
Madrid has turned against bullfighting.
The Pope has got rid of his eunuchs.
A bill was recently passed
to legalize child prostitution.
White faith is beginning to pall
but everything black continues.
The palace of the Antichrist
is ready and waiting, somewhere.
There are intercommunications
between Lesbians and tramps.
It is said that the Wandering Jew
is coming— What else, oh Lord? —

Questions

"Honeybee, what do you know,
you that are all honey and antique gold?
What do you know, Hellenic bee?"
"I know of Pindar."

"Lion with fetid mane,
pensive lion,
perhaps you know of Hercules?"
"Yes. And of Job."

"Viper among the sandalwood
and the lotus, magic viper,
have you worshipped Cleopatra?"
"Yes. And Petronius."

"Rose that the courtesan wore
on her blue silk gown,
have you loved Mary Magdalen?"
"And Jesus, too."

"Scissors that cut off
Samson's hair,
did Samson attract you?"
"No. His woman."

"Whom do you love, white dawn,
white flax, foam, lily,
pure stars? Do you love Abel?"
"No. Cain."

"Eagle, you that are History,
where will you build your nest?
On the peaks of Glory?"
"Yes. In the Mountains of Forgetfulness!"

SECTION EIGHT

from *Poema del otoño y otros poemas*
(Poem of Autumn and Other Poems)

Poem of Autumn

You, with your beard in your hand, meditating,
have you let the best of life escape you, brother?

You grieve for your yesterdays with vain complaints:
there is still the promise of joy in your tomorrows.

You can still seek the lily and the fragrant rose,
and there are still myrtles for your proud, gray head.

The soul, when bored, destroys what it enjoyed,
like Zingua, queen of Angola, black and lustful.

After passing a pleasant hour, you always hear
the ponderous imprecations of Ecclesiastes.

The Sunday of love enchants you; but you watch
the coming of Ash Wednesday; *Memento homo*—

That is why many go toward the flowered mountain;
it also explains Anacreon and Omar Khayyám.

Fleeing from evil, suddenly we enter into evil,
through the wide gates of an artificial paradise.

And yet it is true that life is lovely, for life
includes the pearl, the rose, the star, and woman.

Lucifer gleams. The hoarse ocean sings.
And Silvanus hides behind the trunk of a beech.

We feel that life is pure, and clean, and real,
when wrapped in all the sweetness of the spring.

Why the base jealousies, the base injuries,
when the snakes of pallid furies twist and twine?

Why the benighted hatreds of the ungrateful?
Why those irate grimaces of the Pilates?

Why, if the earth completes both heaven and hell
and our lives are the spindrift of an eternal sea!

Let us wash this bitter tedium from our garments;
let us dream of a mystical rose, a celestial rose.

Let us pluck the flower of the moment, and may the song
of the magic lark express the day's delight!

Love bids us to his feast, and crowns our brows.
Each one of us has a Verona in his life.

At the twilight hour, there is a voice still singing:
"Ruth, with a smile, is coming to glean for Boaz."

Then pluck the flower of the moment, when the dawn
arises in the east for fragrant Youth.

Oh child playing with Eros, oh sprightly children,
dance, oh dance like Grecian nymphs and satyrs.

Old Time gnaws everything, then hastens away;
come, Cynthia and Chloe, come learn to defeat him.

Exchange your roses and orange blossoms, to the sound
of the *Song of Songs* that great Solomon composed.

Priapus watches the gardens where Venus walks;
though Hecate's mastiffs howl, Diana, beautifully

wrapped in the thin white veil of an illusion,
comes down to the groves from heaven to her Endymion.

Youth! Love has the power to change you to gold:
enjoy your kisses in the dawn, oh golden Youth!

How luckless the man who plucks the flower too late!
And alas for the man who has never known love at all!

I have seen, in tropical countries, how the blood
burns in a woman as in a crystal chalice,

and everywhere, women who love and are consumed
like flowers made of flame and of perfume.

Burn, burn, in that flame, and breathe that perfume,
which is the balm for humanity's disorders.

Enjoy the flesh, the blessing that thrills us now
but later will be turned to dust and ashes.

Enjoy the sun, the pagan flare of its fires;
enjoy the sun, for tomorrow you will be blind.

Enjoy the sweet harmonies that invoke Apollo;
enjoy them, for one day you will have no lips.

Enjoy the earth, that proffers us its blessings;
enjoy it, for you soon will lie beneath it.

Forget the fear that cramps and chills your heart;
the dove of Venus is flying over the Sphinx.

Lovers can conquer death and time and fate,
enjoying roses and myrtles in the tomb.

Remember that Anadyomene still aids us,
that naked Phryne reappears in the works of Phidias.

Adam, Biblical but human, is alive and strong,
and we still can taste the apple on our tongues.

And fecundity, universal and omnipotent,
gives force and motion to this living globe.

The heart of heaven is aching for the triumph
of life on earth, which is struggle and is glory.

We grieve and suffer, we quail at the blows of fate,
but the very sap of the universe flows within us.

Our minds contain the vibration of earth and the sun
as a shell on the beach repeats the beat of the sea.

The salt of the sea is plunging through our veins:
our blood is the blood of tritons and of nereids.

Our brows are crowned with live oak and with laurel:
our flesh is the flesh of centaurs and of wood nymphs.

In us, Life becomes force, Life becomes fire.
Let us travel to the land of Death by the path of Love!

Noon

(From "Intermezzo Tropicale")

Midi, roi des étés, as the French creole sang.
Noon is burning the whole island.
The reef is in flames,
the blue sky pours down fire.

This is the island of Cardón, in Nicaragua.
I think of Greece, of Zacynthos or the Peloponnese,
for a tropical Corinth arises before me
in the gleam of the sun and the fondness of the water.

Green plumes of the palm trees. Far off,
rough with antiquity, solemn with myth,
stands the stone tribe of old volcanoes
which, like all else, await their instant of infinity.

A bird of prey flies out to fish, and comes back
with a fish in his talons.
And a sweltering puff of vapor from this oven
turns the cicadas to gold.

Evening

(From "Intermezzo Tropicale")

The siesta hour has passed,
the sunset hour is nearing,
and there is a touch of coolness now
on this sun-stricken tropic coast.
There is a breath of ocean air
and the west pretends to be a forest
lit with a purple flame.

The crabs are marking the sand
with the illegible scrawl of their claws,
and sea shells, color of roses, of gold
reflections, and little snails, and bits
of starfish, are a singing carpet
when you walk these harmonious shores.
And when Venus shines,
imperial love of the godlike evening,
you can hear in the waves the sound
of a lyre or the song of a siren.
And a star like that of Venus glows in my soul.

Saint Helena of Montenegro

Hour of Christ on the cross,
hour of millenial terror,
hour of bloodshed, of the charnel-house.

The moon drips a cold-hearted mood
on the tomb of the Sibyl
and *solvet saeclum in favilla*—

Hecate rages, howling and dark,
and Hell launches its war
through the pustules of the earth.

Medieval hunger stalks
through clouds of sulphurous smoke
and the stench of death. Horror, horror!

The Devil's dogs, in a rage
of envy, bark at the sky
through the mouth of Mongibelo.

Whole peoples tremble in a delirium
of hunger and dread and cold—
Oh God! Oh God! Oh God!

The fears of the Middle Ages,
as in Dante's *Commedia*, besiege us
and our hair stands on end.

Furies pass by with wild gestures,
a thousand twisted faces pass by;
overhead there are disastrous omens.

Throngs of human specters pass by,
gnawing at their hands.
The worms begin their work.

The terrible trumpet is silent,
but the poet's soul can hear
the creaking of the planet's bones.

A vast and unheard sound
is mingled with the earthly noises.
It comes from the unknown.

The crowds of people shout
without faith, without bread, without fire,
maddened by their afflictions.

And Ugolino gnashes
and endlessly gnashes his red
teeth in the darkness of destiny.

And every soul is appalled to see
the phantom of sorrow writhing
between the fire and the miasma.

The Unknown God is frowning,
and Clothos, Lachesis, and Atropos
signal to the Earthquake—

Voices wail and lament;
millionaires and paupers
are equal in their terror.

There are hordes of the suffering,
there are visions of grief and dismay
like those in the Apocalypse.

The heart of the storm
whirls dust about them,
and a divine anger bursts forth.

The ground shifts under their feet
and pain falls on their brows
from the somber skies.

Oh shock and dread of the Muses!
Oh locks of Medusa!
Oh grin of the Empusae!

Oh bitter yellow mask,
eyes shining with a sinister light,
and nightmare scenes!

Bitter dews, a sudden voice
that wounds, and people dying—
Ah! *Miserere!—Miserere!*

Gardens that are graveyards now,
destroyed by the burning irons
of the dreaded mysteries.

Region that fright prefers,
where death is more painful—
Ah! *Miserere!—Miserere!*

But hear that celestial allegro!
For now Saint Helena
is passing among the black horrors.

SECTION NINE

from *Canto a la Argentina y otros poemas*
(Song to the Argentine and Other Poems)

Song to the Argentine

(fragment)

It is the Centennial.
The Plate is a great father:
more than the Tiber and Seine,
more than the fair Thames,
more than the blue Danube
and the Indian Ganges,
it is the mysterious kin
of the biblical Tigris and Euphrates,
for the Adams and Eves of the future
will be born along its shores.
Argentina, land of brothers,
as if to cyclic appeals
you gave a homeland to all
peoples under equal laws;
temples to all religions;
scepters to the sovereigns
who adorn their own brows,
whose own hands crown their heads
with Koh-I-Noors and Regents
polished in their own souls:
those who pour cornucopias,
emperors of seeds,
monarchs of useful labor,
multipliers of bread,
more powerful than Genghis Khan,
greater than Nebuchadnezzer.

The docks bristled with smokestacks;
new ideas and new muscles
landed at the seaports,
sent here by distant nations.

Old rot was scraped away,
false idols and dull weapons
were broken into bits,
and men were linked together
by the fraternity of labor,
the interchange of language.
To offer thanks to God,
the liberal city preserves
the nave of its cathedral,
and the walls of all churches
will rise in every quarter,
all of them equally blest,
the synagogues, the mosques,
the chapels, and the pagodas.
And in this religious flowering,
those who seek light in the darkness,
whether through crescent or swastika,
through the torah or the cross,
will know the nameless God
and find the light they seek.

Traffic, the city's bustle,
clattering iron carriages,
swift steel hippogriffs,
electric roses, flowers
of a thousand and one nights,
Babylonian pomps and trumpets,
the passing of wheels and hooves,
the voice of domestic pianos,
profound human murmurs,
the sound of united voices,
cries and calls, all vibrant
(the pulsing of a taut string),

the feeling of a vital center
like the beat of a great heart
or the breathing of the capital's breast.

Let your proud hymn ring out,
free men of a free land!
Grandsons of the conquistadors,
renewed blood of Spain,
transfused blood of Italy,
of Germany, of the Basques,
and arrivals from the heart
of France and of Great Britain,
life of the Polycolony,
sap of the new fatherland,
of the new Europe that promises
a greater Argentine to come.
Hail, fatherland, for you
are mine and all mankind's!
Hail, in the name of Poetry!
Hail, in the name of Liberty!

SECTION TEN

Miscellaneous Poems

To Amado Nervo

A golden tortoise crawls across the carpet,
and traces on that carpet a mystical stigma;
its carapace is marked with an enigma,
and an enigmatic circle is drawn in its shadow.

Those symbols speak to us of the nameless God
and mark us with his authoritative stigma;
that circle contains the key to the enigma
that slays the Minotaur and dismays Medusa.

Bouquet of dreams, bouquet of ideas that blossomed
in an explosion of songs and a flowering of lives,
you are my gentle breast, my sober thoughts.

And when the silks of the fiesta are gone, tell me
of the subtle effluvia of the orchestra, and of what
is suspended between the violin and the bow.

Knight

I am a semicentaur
with a rough, roguish look.
I imitate the Minotaur
and follow Epicurus.

The laurel on my forehead
predicts my future,
and under the sign of Taurus
I batter down strong walls.

I sing to Proserpina,
who burns hearts
in her smoking brazier.

I am Satan, and I am Christ
dying between two thieves—
Oh where do I exist?

Nicaraguan Triptych

I The Clowns

I remember two dwarfs, back there in our country home,
two dwarfs like those of Velázquez. One was a man
they called The Captain. The other, his old companion,
was his mother. And they looked as if they were brothers.

They were like straw men, like specters, like caterpillars.
The Captain limped, he was cross-eyed, he made wild faces;
he used to fashion dolls and small wax figures
with his short, puffy, horrible little fingers.

At times he played he was a bishop, and blessed us all;
the sermons he preached were devilishly complex;
he said the Pater Noster and the Ave Maria.

Then the two dwarfs would quietly leave the room,
and while the country people were all laughing,
I, silent in a corner, was afraid.

II Eros

It is the time of my youth, my youth that plays
with rhymes and illusions, a golden sword at its hip;
my mind holds a dream always different and distinct,
and my agile spirit surrenders itself to chance—

I see in every woman a Grecian nymph;
I paint their charm and grace in sonorous poems;
and then this passes to love of the port of Corinth,
or of Chinandega, rich in succulent oranges.

That time is far off now. But I still see blossoms
on the green, aromatic trees in the orange grove;
or the old ships arriving from distant lands;

or the cocoa plum; or the clustered mangrove trees;
or you, the face I adored in that time, looking
out at me with a first love or a first repentence.

III *Earthquake*

Daybreak. The great town reposes in its silence.
As a child, I listened to tales and counsels there,
or attended serenades under the barred window
of some young, simple, God-fearing, lovely sweetheart.

The constellations still glitter in the sky,
but there is a soft pink light on the Eastern horizon—
when suddenly an earthquake shakes the old houses,
and the people kneel to pray in the streets and patios,

half-naked, crying: "Dear God! Immortal God!"
The earth trembles each moment, as if it were shaken
by some invisible and apocalyptic hand—

The air is heavy as lead. There is no wind.
And it could be said that Death has passed this way
under the impassivity of the firmament.

The Victory of Samothrace

Her vanished head still speaks of that sacred day
on which the glorying multitude paraded
in the winds of triumph before the simulacrum;
the day when victory filled the streets of Athens.

This figure has no eyes, and yet it sees;
no mouth, and yet it utters the supreme cry;
no arms, and yet it sets the whole lyre singing;
and its great marble wings embrace the infinite.

Christmas Sonnet

Mary was pale, and Joseph the carpenter also:
they saw in the eyes of that pure and lovely face
the heavenly miracle which the star announced
and the martyrdom that was waiting for the lamb.

The shepherds sang very softly, and at the last
a car of archangels left a shining track;
the light of Aldebaran could hardly be seen,
and even the morning star was late to appear.

This vision rises within me, and multiplies
in gorgeous details, in a thousand rich marvels,
because of the sure hope of most divine good

of the Virgin, the Child, and outlawed Saint Joseph;
and I, on my poor donkey, ride toward Egypt,
with no star any longer, and far from Bethlehem.

Pax

(fragment)

It was the year 1870.
France was racked by a cruel war.
Hugo wrote it out in his poems.

And Paris, that divine city,
all celebrating stilled, could see
only shadows on Christmas Eve,

and these were the siege, and hunger,
and dread, and hate, and harm.
All was death, or ruin, or lust.

On one side of the Seine, the ready
might of conquering Germany;
on the other, unready France.

The bells of Notre Dame
rang twelve: the magic hour
that foretells a mystical dawn.

And on the left bank of the Seine
a Christmas Eve *noel*
arose from the heavy shadows.

A silence. And then that fierce army
answered, nobly, austerely,
with a solemn hymn by Luther.

And in the vast night of war,
Christ, who banishes hatred,
cast out evil through song.

Is there no one of a younger race
who can shatter war's yoke
and unite Beethoven's power
with the songs Hugo bequeathed us?

1915

Paternoster to Pan

Our father, ambiguous father
of the eternal miracles
that we moderns admire because
of your great and ancient fame.

The nymph passes by the fountain,
and her whiteness includes
what inspires, what perdures,
what perfumes, and what provokes.

For on seeing the living flower
or the statue that moves,
made all of roses and snow,
our souls are captured by love.

Our Pan, which art on earth
because the universe might take fright,
hallowed be thy name
for all that it signifies.

Bring us back your joyous kingdom
in which you come singing
with the throngs of bacchantes
crashing through the thickets.

You are always violently alive;
with your wild impulsiveness,
shake your celestial horns in the sky,
sink your goat's feet in the earth.

Give us rhythm and measure
through the love of your song;
and through the love of your flute, give us
this day our daily love.

The debts the loving soul incurs
are in your hands,
and do not grant forgiveness
to him who has never loved.

Sadly, Very Sadly—

Once I was sadly, very sadly watching
the waters of a fountain rise and fall back.
It was at night, at a soft and silver hour.
The night wept. The night sighed. The night
sobbed. And daybreak diluted in its gentle
amethyst the tears of a mysterious artist.
And that artist was myself, mysterious, moaning,
mingling my soul with the waters of the fountain.

EPILOGUE

A Speech *Al Alimón* on Rubén Darío

by FEDERICO GARCÍA LORCA

and PABLO NERUDA

A Speech *Al Alimón* on Rubén Darío

(Pen Club, Buenos Aires, 1933)

Neruda: Ladies...

García Lorca: And gentlemen. There is a pass in bullfighting called *al alimón,* in which two bullfighters cite the bull while grasping either side of the same cape.

Neruda: Federico and I, tied together by an electric wire, are going to act together in response to this very impressive reception.

García Lorca: It is customary, at meetings like this, for a poet to offer his living words, whether silver or wooden, and to greet his friends and colleagues with his own voice.

Neruda: But we are going to set up a dead man among you, a widower companion, obscure in the darkness of a death greater than other deaths; life's widower, who in his day was a dazzling husband. We are going to hide under his fiery shadow, we are going to repeat his name until his power leaps out of forgetfulness.

García Lorca: After we have sent our embraces, with the tenderness of penguins, to that delicate poet Amado Villar, we are going to fling a great name onto the table, with the assurance that the glasses will break, that the forks will jump up and seek the eyes they long for, and that a crash of the sea will stain the tablecloth. We are going to name the poet of America and Spain: Rubén...

Neruda: Darió. Because, ladies...

García Lorca: And gentlemen...

Neruda: Where in Buenos Aires is the Rubén Darío Plaza?

García Lorca: Where is there a statue of Rubén Darío?

Neruda: He loved parks. Where is the Rubén Darío Park?

García Lorca: Where is the Rubén Darío Florist Shop?

Neruda: Where is the apple tree, where are the apples, named after Rubén Darío?

García Lorca: Where is the mummified hand of Rubén Darío?

Neruda: Where are the oil, the resin, and the swan with the name of Rubén Darío?

García Lorca: Rubén Darío sleeps in his "native Nicaragua," under a frightful mock-marble lion like those lions the rich put at the front doors of their houses.

Neruda: A drugstore lion, for one who was a creator of lions. A starless lion, for one who consecrated stars.

García Lorca: He gave us the murmur of the forest in an adjective, and being a master of language, like Fray Luis de Granada, he made zodiacal signs out of the lemon tree, the hoof of a stag, and mollusks full of terror and infinity. He launched us on the sea with frigates and shadows in our eyes, and built an enormous promenade of gin over the grayest afternoon the sky has ever known, and greeted the southwest wind as a friend, all heart like a Romantic poet, and put his hand on the Corinthian capital of all epochs with a sad, ironic doubt.

Neruda: His red name deserves to be remembered, along with his essential tendencies, his terrible heartaches, his incandescent uncertainties, his descent to the hospitals of hell, his ascent to the castles of fame, his attributes as a great poet, now and forever undeniable.

García Lorca: As a Spanish poet he taught the old and the young in Spain with a generosity and a sense of universality that are lacking in the poets of today. He taught Valle-Inclán and Juan Ramón Jiménez and the Machado brothers, and his voice was water and niter in the furrows of our venerable language. From Rodrigo Caro to the Argensolas or Don Juan

Arguijo, Spanish had not seen such plays on words, such clashes of consonants, such lights and forms, as in Rubén Darío. From the landscapes of Velázquez and Goya's bonfire and Quevedo's melancholy to the elegant apple color of the Mallorcan peasant girls, Darío walked the Spanish earth as in his own land.

Neruda: He brought a tide to Chile, the hot northern sea, and he left that sea there, abandoned on the hard, rock-toothed coast, and the ocean battered it with spume and bells, and the black winds of Valparaíso filled it with sonorous salt. Tonight let us carve his statue out of air, crisscrossed with smoke and voices, with circumstances, with life, like his own magnificent poetry, crisscrossed with sounds and dreams.

García Lorca: But I want this statue of air to show his blood, like a branch of coral shaken by the tide; his nerves, like a photograph of sheet-lightning; his minotaur's head, where the Gongoresque snow is painted by a flight of humming-birds; his vague, absent eyes, the eyes of a millionaire whose millions are tears; and also his defects: the weeds and the empty flute notes in his book-shelves, and the cognac bottles of his dramatic drunkenness, and the impudent padding that fills the multitude of his lines with humanity. The fertile substance of his great poetry stands solidly outside of norms, forms, and schools.

Neruda: Federico García Lorca, a Spaniard, and I, a Chilean, dedicate the honors bestowed on us today to that great shadow who sang more loftily than ourselves, and who saluted, in a new voice, the Argentinian soil that we now tread.

García Lorca: Pablo Neruda, a Chilean, and I, a Spaniard, are one in our language and one in our reverence for that great Nicaraguan, Argentinian, Chilean, and Spanish poet Rubén Darío.

Neruda and García Lorca: In whose honor, and to whose glory, we raise our glass.

Index of Titles in Spanish and English